DISCOVERING OUR HERITAGE

EL SALVADOR

ON THE ROAD TO PEACE

BY KAREN SCHWABACH

DILLON PRESS

PARSIPPANY, NEW JERSEY

Acknowledgments

The author would like to thank Aaron Schwabach for information about immigration law, Deborah Schwabach for technical assistance, the Guevara family for their hospitality and assistance, the students and teachers of the Escuela Dr. Camilo Arevalo in Los Naranjos, Vitelio's English class at Instituto Cultural Oxford in San Salvador, the teachers at Cuzcatlan Language School in San Salvador, and especially the school director, Eduardo Guevara, for his information about Salvadoran humor and folk beliefs, his assistance, and his boundless patience. Thanks to all of the Salvadoran people who shared their stories with me and helped me find my way around their beautiful country.

Photo Credits
Front cover: *l.* Chris R. Sharp/D. Donne Bryant Stock Photography; *m.* Jose Canas; *r.* Luis Romero/AP/Wide World Photos

AP/Wide World Photos/Luis Romero: 63. Jose Canas: 19, 117.
D. Donne Bryant Stock Photography: 11; Alyx Kellington: 49; John Mitchell: 36; Chris R. Sharp: 8. Ken Heyman: 54. Impact Visuals/Donna DeCesare: 44, 48, 65, 83, 109. Karen Schwabach: 14, 15, 17, 18, 20, 25, 29, 38, 51, 75, 77, 81, 89, 92, 94, 101, 103. Silver Burdett Ginn: 5 t., b. Kathy Sloane: 33. The Viesti Collection/Joe Viesti: 69.

Map and flag by Ortelius Design.

Library of Congress Cataloging-in-Publication Data
Schwabach, Karen.
    El Salvador : on the road to peace / by Karen Schwabach.
        p. cm.—(Discovering our heritage)
    Includes bibliographical references (p.   ) and index.
    Summary: Describes the land, people, history, legends and folk tales, festivals and holidays, and everyday life of El Salvador.
    1. El Salvador—Juvenile literature. [1. El Salvador.]
I. Title. II. Series
F1483.2.S4 1999
972.84—dc21   97-37278

ISBN 0-382-39453-4 (LSB)
10 9 8 7 6 5 4 3 2 1

Cover and book design by Michelle Farinella

 Dillon Press
A Division of Simon & Schuster
299 Jefferson Road, P.O. Box 480
Parsippany, NJ   07054-0480

CONTENTS

Fast Facts About El Salvador

Official Name: República de El Salvador (Republic of El Salvador)

Capital: San Salvador

Location: Central America; bordered by Guatemala on the north and northwest, the Pacific Ocean on the south, and Honduras on the north and east

Area: 8,260 square miles (21,392 square kilometers), about the size of Massachusetts

Elevation: *Highest*—Monte Cristo, 7,933 feet (2,418 meters); *Lowest*—sea level along the coast

Population: 5,828,987 (1996 estimate)

Form of Government: Republic; *Head of State*—president

Important Products: *Agriculture*—coffee, cotton, sugar cane, corn, beans, fruit, rice, cattle, pigs; *Forestry*—balsam; *Manufacturing*—textiles, clothing, shoes, food, cement, petroleum products

Basic Unit of Money: Colon (1996 value about 12.5 U.S. cents)

Official Language: Spanish

Major Religions: About 70 percent Roman Catholic; 30 percent Baptist, Pentecostal, and other Christian groups

Flag: Three horizontal stripes; the outer stripes are blue; the middle stripe is white with the seal of El Salvador

National Anthems: "Himno Nacional" ("The National Hymn")

Major Holidays: New Year's Day—January 1; Holy Week—March or April; Independence Day—September 15; Day of the Dead (also called All Souls' Day)—November 2; Christmas—December 25 (celebrated December 24–31)

THE LAND OF
PRECIOUS THINGS

Long ago El Salvador was known as *Cuzcatlán*, a word in the Nahuatlan language that means "the land of precious things" or "the land of happiness." There are no jewels or gold to be found in El Salvador, but there are many other precious things—high green mountains, waterfalls, the tall cones of volcanoes, and bright blue volcanic lakes. There are the Montecristo Cloud Forest, where dozens of bird species make their home, and high rock cliffs from which you can see across miles of green valley to the white breakers of the sea.

El Salvador is on the Pacific coast of Central America, between Guatemala and Honduras. The country stands at the meeting point of three of the plates that form the earth's crust. The movement of the plates causes earthquakes and volcanic activity. There are more than 20 volcanoes in El Salvador. There are also tremors, or small earthquakes, every few weeks. Usually the tremors make the furniture in houses tremble, and rattle the tin roofs, but cause no damage.

El Salvador is near the equator, so it has a tropical climate. There are only two seasons—*invierno* ("winter"), the rainy season from mid-May to mid-October, and *verano* ("summer"), the dry season. During invierno it rains

almost every day, and many roads in rural areas turn to mud. But even with the rainfall, the temperatures remain very hot, except in the mountains.

El Salvador is about the size of the state of Massachusetts and is home to almost 6 million people. Because the country is so small, every bit of available land is valuable. For that reason, crops are planted on the sides of steep mountains instead of just in the valleys. Land is expensive and hard to get. Most of the land belongs to a few very rich families. This unfair system of land ownership was the main cause of El Salvador's civil war, which began in 1980 and ended in 1992.

The war was between the FMLN (Farabundo Martí National Liberation Front), who wanted to change the way land was owned, and the government's army. The war lasted 12 years and disrupted the lives of Salvadorans in many ways. One fourth of the Salvadoran people had to flee their homes, moving to other parts of El Salvador, or to Honduras, Mexico, or the United States. More than 75,000 people died, and thousands of others disappeared. Buildings, bridges, and communication systems were destroyed, and the economy suffered. Years of rebuilding and recovery lie ahead.

A Spanish-Speaking Country

El Salvador is one of the world's many Spanish-

One of El Salvador's many tall volcanoes

speaking countries. Spanish, which comes from Latin, was brought to the Americas by the Spaniards, who conquered most of what is now called Latin America—South America, Central America, and the Spanish-speaking nations of the Caribbean. Like most of the other Latin American nations, El Salvador was once ruled by Spain. Some Latin Americans refer to themselves as Latinos.

The people of El Salvador are descended from Europeans, Pipíl Indians, and a small number of Africans who were brought to the country as slaves. About 5 percent of the population still consider themselves Pipíl Indians, living in villages where native customs are practiced. But only about 150 people still speak the Nahuatlan language of the Pipíl.

El Occidente—The West

Coffee plantations or farms—called *fincas*—occupy the steep green mountains in the western part of El Salvador. The rows of coffee bushes climb up the high mountains and descend into the narrow valleys separated by rows of tall trees, which protect the delicate bushes from the wind and the sun. Coffee that is grown above 3,500 feet is of higher quality. Coffee is El Salvador's main export. It takes a lot of land to grow coffee and a lot of people to tend, harvest, and process the beans.

The cathedral in Santa Ana

El Salvador's second largest city is also in the western part of the country. It is called *la bella Santa Ana* ("the beautiful Santa Ana") because of its tree-lined streets, parks, plazas, and its cathedral.

Two of El Salvador's national parks are also in this region. Salvadorans visit Cerro Verde National Park to see the deep-blue waters of Lake Coatepeque and to climb Santa Ana, which is the largest volcano in the country and still active. (An active volcano is a volcano that might erupt again.) Izalco is another volcano in the park. This mountain did not exist until 1770, when a small hole in a field began to erupt. By 1966, when the eruptions stopped, the lava flowing from the hole had formed a cone of bare rock 6,234 feet (1900 meters) high.

Montecristo National Park is part of a cloud forest that surrounds El Trifinio, the mountain peak where Guatemala, Honduras, and El Salvador meet. All three countries have national parks in the forest. More than 6.5 feet (2 meters) of rain falls on the forest every year. The tree growth is so dense that little sunlight reaches the ground, and the forest drips with moisture. Mosses and orchids flourish in the dark, damp forest. This special ecosystem is home to almost 100 species of birds, including hummingbirds and toucans. Deer, foxes, porcupines, spider monkeys, and jaguars also live in the cloud forest.

Also in the West is Joya de Cerén, the ruins of an ancient village that was buried by a volcano about 1,500 years ago. The site was discovered in 1976 by a bulldozer operator. Archaeologists have been able to learn about the daily lives of El Salvador's early inhabitants by studying the homes in the village. Tools, eating utensils, and even food have been found where people must have left them as they fled the volcanic eruption. It is believed that no one was killed in the eruption.

El Oriente—The East

Like the West, the East has many coffee fincas. Much of eastern El Salvador is mountainous. Along the coast are black sand beaches where Salvadoran families come to swim and surfers come to ride the high waves. The cities of San Vicente, San Miguel, and the port city of La Unión are the largest cities of the region.

San Miguel and San Vicente, like many Salvadoran cities, were built at the foot of volcanoes. It is dangerous to live beside a volcano, but the volcanic soil is fertile and so is the best for growing crops. La Unión was a port for 300 years until it closed down during the recent civil war.

Most of the fighting in the civil war occurred in the East. The government army kept control of the West throughout the war, but in the East there were constant battles for towns and land. Today the East bears more scars from the war than the West.

San Salvador

In the Plaza Barrios, a large square in the center of San Salvador, crowds of people gather on weekends to talk, walk, and enjoy the sunshine. Clowns perform tricks and skits while street vendors sell fruits, soft drinks, and ice cream. Sometimes a man or woman, microphone in hand, makes a religious or political speech to anyone who will listen.

A crowd gathers to watch a clown perform in the Plaza Barrios.

Towering over the square is the still unfinished Metropolitan Cathedral, which was heavily damaged in the 1986 earthquake that rocked San Salvador. Other important buildings, including the National Museum and the National Library, were also damaged in the earthquake and have not yet been repaired.

Near the Plaza Barrios is the Mercado Central, a huge market, which begins in a large building and spreads out over several downtown streets. Some streets are completely filled with double rows of market stalls so that traffic no longer

A market in San Salvador

passes down them. Tin roofs over the streets protect vendors and shoppers from the frequent rains during invierno. Almost anything anybody needs or wants is for sale at the Mercado Central—food, clothes, shoes, schoolbooks, toys, barrels for storing water, cylindrical blocks of blue soap for washing clothes and dishes, basins and tubs for bathing, electric fans, music tapes and compact discs, hammers, saws and machetes, colorful blankets and clothing from Guatemala, packets of pills and bottles of medicine and bundles of herbs to cure almost anything.

The central part of the city is always crowded. Shoppers have to walk very carefully, because the sidewalks are so busy that they sometimes have to step into the streets to let other people pass. The streets are even busier. There are plenty of buses—a bus comes every minute or two on most of the city's routes—and more and more Salvadorans are buying cars. All of this traffic produces a lot of pollution and many accidents. Drivers sometimes get frustrated and fail to stop for red lights.

Much of El Salvador's small middle class live in San Salvador, in neighborhoods of beautiful old stone buildings damaged by the 1986 earthquake and the civil war. The rich live in the western part of the city, where the famous Zona Rosa is located. The Zona Rosa is a business district of chic, upscale boutiques and restaurants where the very wealthy shop and dine, often paying for their purchases in U.S. dollars. In the neighborhoods near the Zona Rosa, luxurious houses are hidden behind high walls and iron gates and are guarded by private police forces. Not far away is a field where squatters live in shelters constructed of sheet plastic and scrap lumber. The squatters are people who have moved to San Salvador from the countryside and can't find or can't afford to rent apartments. Recently the rich people tried to remove the squatters from the field but were not successful. Most of the people in San Salvador sided with the squatters.

A middle class neighborhood in San Salvador

The Government

El Salvador is a republic, with an 84-member legislative assembly and a president elected by the people. The constitution says that a president is elected for a five-year term and cannot be reelected. In reality the military is more powerful than the elected government. Most presidents have been members of the military, and several times the military has overthrown elected presidents.

Families from the countryside use anything they can find to build houses in San Salvador.

The country is divided into 14 departments. Each department has a governor appointed by the national government. Each department is divided into *cantones*, or rural divisions, and *ciudades*, or cities. The ciudades and some of the cantones have elected mayors.

Transportation

Most Salvadorans travel on the inexpensive and efficient

The colorfully painted buses are usually overloaded with riders.

bus system. The buses run frequently from San Salvador to every part of the city and the country. In the city, riders never have to wait more than a few minutes for a bus, and the ride costs only a few cents. Buses to the countryside also run very often, and travelers can go almost anywhere in the country for less than three U.S. dollars.

Most of the buses are old U.S. schoolbuses from the 1950s, 60s, and 70s. Drivers like to personalize their buses by painting the names of their friends on the outside and

El Salvador's international airport

adding religious pictures or messages. Inside they decorate with colorful plastic strings, yarn, and stickers so that each bus is a little different from the others.

El Salvador has many good roads and highways, and in the last few years, many Salvadorans have bought cars. But often those who own cars prefer to ride the bus. It is cheaper than driving and easier than worrying about the traffic or finding a parking space. In the countryside, people usually walk on short trips. Most country roads are full of walkers all day long. Drivers toot their horns before driving into a village to warn the walkers that a car is coming.

El Salvador's international airport, completed in 1979, has a modern terminal decorated with Maya-style carvings. Far away from any city or town, it was built near the beaches because the government hoped that the country would soon have a busy tourism industry. Almost every flight that enters or leaves the airport is full. But the flights are filled with people coming from the United States to visit relatives in El Salvador or leaving El Salvador to visit relatives in the United States. There are very few tourists.

Farming and Manufacturing

Tracts of land for farming are divided into three types: *haciendas*, large tracts for growing coffee; *latifundios*, large tracts for growing other crops; and *minifundios*, small tracts for growing corn, rice, beans, and other foods. El Salvador's main exports are coffee, sugar, and cotton. Corn, beans, and rice—staple foods—and fruits and vegetables are produced for sale inside the country. About 40 percent of the nation's workers are involved in agriculture. The minimum wage for agricultural workers is about $2.50 a day.

Factory workers are paid a little more than that, which makes factory work appealing to many people. During the 1970s the government established the Zona Franca, or "free zone," where foreign companies could build factories without paying taxes to the government. A piece of clothing that says "Made in El Salvador" probably came from the free zone. Workers in the free zone earn about 56 cents an hour. This is about one fifth of what it costs to support a family of four in El Salvador. Because there is little government control over the factories, the managers sometimes abuse their workers—requiring them to work many extra hours without pay or even beating them. If the workers refuse, they lose their jobs. Much of the clothing produced in these factories is sold in the United States. Recently one U.S. clothing chain decided to stop selling clothing made in the free zone until the factories start treating their workers better.

El Medio Ambiente—The Environment

Like people all over the world, Salvadorans are concerned about preserving the natural beauty of their country. This means teaching people to take care of the national parks. It also means trying to clean up polluted rivers and lakes. Now that the civil war is over, Salvadorans are beginning to study the country's environmental problems and discuss solutions.

In 1996, volunteers began planting a Reconciliation Forest on Guazapa Volcano, which had been deforested by bombs during the war. By the time the project is completed, 75,000 trees will have been planted, one for each person killed in the war. In the summer of 1996, the nation's first environmental conference was held in San Salvador.

Most of the country's 300 rivers are polluted, and air pollution is also a serious problem, especially in San Salvador. Salvadorans feel strongly that it is important to begin work on these problems.

THE SALVADORANS

The Spanish name for the Salvadorans is los Salvadoreños. There are about six million Salvadorans. Only a few Salvadoran people—about one in ten—are middle class, and even fewer are rich. But some people in El Salvador are very, very rich. The fincas, where many Salvadorans work, belong to very rich people.

People who work on the fincas or live in the country-side are called *campesinos*, which means "country people" or "peasants." Today more and more people are moving to the cities to work in factories or businesses. But even after they move to the city, people are still proud to think of themselves as campesinos.

A Religious People

El Salvador is Spanish for "the Savior." Most people in El Salvador are Christians. Christians believe that Jesus Christ, who was born about 2,000 years ago, was the son of God and came to this world to save people from evil. The country is thus named after the Savior.

Religion is very important to most Salvadoran people. People wear religious symbols, paint religious messages on their cars, and name their businesses after religious

A church in the village of Los Naranjos

ideas or important saints. When people meet on the street, they often say *"Dios le bendiga"* ("God bless you") as a greeting. Most people in El Salvador are Catholic, but more and more people are joining other Christian groups.

Many of the Catholics and other Christian groups follow liberation theology, a religious movement that started in Latin America during the 1960s. Liberation theologists believe that people need to be liberated, or freed, from the rich people who oppress them. The rich also need to be freed from the system of oppression. For this liberation to happen, there needs to be a change in the way that people own things—in El Salvador and elsewhere. All people need to share in the ownership of land, factories, and other means of production that now belong to rich people.

To work together to make these changes, some liberation theologists live together in places called Christian Base Communities. During the recent civil war, some communities disappeared because their members left to join the FMLN or were killed by the government. Other communities are still working to gain freedom for Salvadoran people.

Working Hard and Helping Others

In addition to their religion, most Salvadorans place a high value on hard work, close family ties, and being kind to others. People in other countries consider Salvadorans to be very hard workers, and many Salvadorans believe that it is easier for them to get a job in the United States because of this reputation. They believe that if they work hard enough, they will be well off. They say, "I was born poor, but I don't have to die poor."

Many Salvadorans get up early in the morning and often clean the house or do other chores before eating breakfast and going to work. Even though unemployment is high, people find ways to work. If they don't have jobs, they make lunches to sell to people who do have jobs, or they sell refreshments on the buses. Many people run small businesses in their homes.

Most Salvadorans also place a high value on caring for their families. People feel a strong responsibility to their families—parents to children, children to parents, and brothers and sisters to each other. It is important to help other family members.

Salvadorans consider it important to be kind and helpful to strangers as well as to friends and family. People often help others on the streets and on the buses. When someone carrying a heavy load gets off a bus, people will help the person down, hand him or her the load, and call to the driver to wait until the person is off the bus. People who have a seat on a crowded bus hold the bags and bundles of those who are standing.

Generosity is also important in El Salvador's culture. Salvadorans believe in being generous not only to their family and friends, but also to people who ask for money on the street.

Like people everywhere, Salvadorans love to laugh. They like clowns, jokes, cartoons, and funny stories. They say that to be a real Salvadoran, a person must be ready to tell a good joke whenever asked.

Social Life

In the countryside the most important social events usually happen at the churches. Sometimes the churches will have a week-long revival with prayer meetings, musicians, and preaching every night. Young people may go to

the church service, or they may prefer to stay outside, talking to their friends, listening to the music, and eating the
food that the church women cook and sell in the church-
yard. If more than one church is holding a revival, the
young people walk from one church to another to see what
is going on. If there are no church events, people often
walk up and down the main street or around the main plaza
in the evening, meeting and talking to friends.

In San Salvador, people enjoy going to the city parks on
weekends. Families take picnics, and young couples stroll
along the walkways together. Everyone enjoys getting away
from the noise and pollution of the city for a few hours. At
the Parque Infantil there are rides, playgrounds, and environmental education displays for children as well as botani-
cal gardens and quiet areas for older people to enjoy.

Whether going to church, to the park, or just walking
around, Salvadorans feel it's important to dress well. Most
people wear the best clothes they can afford whenever they
leave the house. It's common to see children playing in the
park who look as though they're dressed for a wedding.

Casas de la Cultura

In many towns and villages, the Casa de la Cultura, or
"house of culture," is an important gathering place. The houses
are sponsored by the government's Ministry of Education and

Families enjoy a train ride in Parque Infantil, San Salvador.

provide public libraries, classes, and cultural activities. At some houses there are folk-dance classes; lessons in weaving, pottery, painting, and traditional medicine; and public readings by poets and novelists. In communities where traditional dances and festivals are disappearing, workers at the Casa de la Cultura try to revive them.

More than 100 Casas de la Cultura have been started in El Salvador in the last 20 years. The houses are so popular that even during the civil war, the number kept growing. The government plans to provide more communities with cultural centers in the future.

Communications

Many Salvadoran families have a television set or know somebody who does. There are no Salvadoran TV shows except for news broadcasts, but *telenovelas* ("soap operas") from Mexico, comedies from other Spanish-speaking countries, and some shows from the United States are popular.

El Salvador has more than 60 radio stations that play popular songs from all over Latin America. *Radio Venceremos* ("Radio We Shall Overcome"), which was an FMLN-operated radio station during the civil war, is now one of San Salvador's popular radio stations.

San Salvador has several daily newspapers, which usually print what the government wants them to print. They report on many problems, especially crime, but they rarely report on problems in the government. Large sections of each paper are filled with social notes about birthday parties, tea parties, and baby showers that rich people have had.

Many families have telephones. Telephones are expensive, but sometimes several households will get together to have one installed. An extension is then installed in each house. In some villages there is only one telephone number, but each family has an extension. People who don't have telephones can have their friends and relatives telephone them at a neighbor's house. Most Salvadorans have relatives in the United States and want to be able to get in touch quickly in case of an emergency. The government owns the telephone company, ANTEL, but is planning to sell it to private investors. Salvadorans are worried about this change because they think it will become even more expensive to have a telephone.

El Salvador's Writers

El Salvador has many famous novelists and poets. The most famous Salvadoran writer is Salarué, whose real name is Salvador Salazar Arrué. His best-known book, *Cuentos de Barro (Tales of Mud)*, tells about peasant life in El Salvador. Maria Lopez Viagíl is another important author. Neither author's work has been translated into English.

El Salvador's poets include Claudia Lars (whose real name is Carmen Brannon de Samayoa Chincilla), Oswaldo Escobar Velado, Claribel Alegría, and Roque Dalton. Many of Alegría's books, including *Ashes of Izalco* and *Flowers from the Volcano*, have been translated into English.

Dalton, whose poems were often political, was a member of the FMLN. In 1975 he was shot by his comrades because they believed he was an American spy. One of his books, *Clandestine Poems*, has been published in English.

Manlio Argueta's recent children's book, *Magic Dogs of the Volcanoes*, retells a Salvadoran folk tale in Spanish and English. It has been published in the United States.

Art

Bright, colorful paintings on wood are El Salvador's best-known art form. The pictures usually show religious figures or scenes from rural life. This style of painting was made popular by an artist named Fernando Llort, from the village of La Palma. Many other artists in La Palma now paint similar pictures, and the style is called La Palma painting.

José Mejía Vides is a painter whose pictures show Salvadoran village life. Noé Canjura, Julia Díaz, Camilio Minero, Victor Manuel Sanabri, and Luis Angel Salinas are other well-known artists.

Salvadoran folk art includes weaving, ceramics, pottery, hammock making, and embroidery. Tiny clay figurines, embroidered clothing, and brightly colored blankets are made in the countryside by artisans and sold in the markets of the large cities.

Music

Because Spanish is spoken in so many countries, the

This brightly colored embroidery is an example of Salvadoran folk art.

same bands and songs are usually popular throughout Latin America. Some favorite Latin American music and dance styles are cúmbia, salsa, and merengue. Many radio stations also play hits from the United States. Because most Salvadorans are Christians, contemporary Christian music is also very popular.

Folk music is played on the guitar and on traditional wooden pipes. Some folk songs are so old that nobody remembers who wrote them. Political problems, the civil war, and peace are often subjects of newer songs.

The Road to Peace

During the civil war, daily life changed, and the Salvadoran people changed. It was dangerous to leave the house. If a family member was gone longer than expected, the family organized a search party. Almost every family lost some members during the war. Many people got into the habit of telephoning their relatives every hour to make sure they were all right. Some people still do this. There are Salvadorans who still have difficulty sleeping at night. A few are frightened by the sound of planes and helicopters. Some do not leave their houses after dark. In areas where there was a lot of fighting during the war, people do not take evening walks.

But the Salvadorans are glad that their country is on the road to peace. They feel freer and less frightened than they felt in the past. People feel that life is much better than it was and that it is getting better all the time. People talk about *consolidar la paz,* or "making the peace solid." They know there is a lot of work ahead to repair the damage done to the country and its people during 12 years of war. But the Salvadoran people are hard workers, and they know they can do it.

EL SALVADOR'S HISTORY

Nobody is sure when humans first came to live in the land now called El Salvador. Both the Maya and the Aztecs lived in Central America and Mexico, and both groups probably lived in El Salvador at one time. Historians disagree about whether the Maya or the Aztecs were the ancestors of the Pipíl who came to inhabit El Salvador. The Pipíl, like the Aztecs, spoke a dialect of the Nahuatlan language. But their society was organized into large city-states, like those of the Maya. As archaeologists study the ruins at Tazumál and Joya de Cerén, they may be able to tell us more about the first humans in El Salvador.

The Pipíl of Cuzcatlán were farmers. They grew corn, beans, root vegetables, cocoa, gourds, fruit, cotton, hemp, bamboo, and tobacco. Most people belonged to the *macehualtín* class, people who farmed land. Land belonged to everybody, and everybody had a share in what was produced. Not everybody did the same amount of work, though. There were nobles, who didn't have to do any work. There were warriors, who had slaves to work their pieces of land for them. There were merchants, who traveled to other lands to buy and sell goods and to spy for the warriors. There was the chief, who decided which families would farm which plots of land. But the warriors

Maya ruins at Tazumál

chose the chief and had more power than the other classes.

An Invasion From the East

In 1493 in Rome, Pope Alexander VI, the leader of the Roman Catholic Church, gave orders that would change the Pipíls' lives forever. He said that King Ferdinand and Queen Isabella of Spain had the absolute right to any land that was discovered west of the Azores and Cape Verde Islands in the eastern Atlantic Ocean. The king and queen sent explorers to find these lands, to discover if there were any gold and jewels there, and to figure out other ways to get wealth from the lands. They were also supposed to turn the people of these lands into Christians.

Cuzcatlán did not have any gold or silver, so the invaders didn't bother to attack it until 1524. From Mexico, Hernán Cortés sent an army of 5,000 Aztecs and 250 Spanish soldiers across the Paz River into Cuzcatlán. But the Pipíl were expecting them. Even though the invaders had guns and swords and the Pipíl didn't even have metal tools, the war over Cuzcatlán lasted 15 years. In the end the Pipíl lost.

The invaders divided the land into *encomiendas*. A European who was granted an encomienda by the king and queen of Spain was also given the Pipíl who lived on the land. The Pipíl had to work for him, and he was responsible for protecting them and teaching them to be Christians.

The Pipíl did not want to become Christians because they already had a religion. They worshiped Quetzalcoatl, the newborn sun; Tlaloc, the rain; Tonatiuh, the adult sun; and Metzi, the moon. To help them change their minds, the Christians destroyed the temples and images of these gods. Many of the invaders believed that if the Pipíl refused to be baptized as Christians, it was better to kill them. Not everyone agreed. One Catholic priest, Bartolome de las Casas, said "I prefer a live unbaptized Indian to a dead Christian one."

The Pipíl had always grown the things they needed for

This Catholic church in Panchimalco was built in 1725.

themselves, but the new landowners wanted to make money. They made the Pipíl plant indigo, which yields a blue dye that sold for a high price in Europe but was dangerous to grow. Many Pipíl died from illnesses caused by growing indigo. As the seventeenth and eighteenth centuries passed, there were fewer and fewer Pipíl and more and more *mestizos*, who were a mixture of the Pipíl and Europeans.

Independence

Because Central America consisted of colonies ruled by Spain, the king and queen of Spain controlled the indigo trade. The Europeans who had been born in Central

America, called creoles, didn't care about the king and queen. They wanted to be independent so that they could make more money from the indigo. In 1821, all of the Central American colonies except Panama declared their independence from Spain. Later they formed a new federation called the United Provinces of Central America. El Salvador was part of it.

But many people were unhappy in the new federation. Taxes were high and more and more land was being taken by the rich. Life was very difficult for the campesinos, the Pipíl and mestizos who worked the land. The Pipíl, under the leadership of Anastasio Aquino, rebelled against the government and took back some land. They declared an independent territory, Tepitán. The government army invaded Tepitán and put down the rebellion. The rich people learned that they needed the military to help them keep what they had.

The federation began to collapse in 1838. Unsure what to do, the leaders of El Salvador asked the United States Congress to admit El Salvador to the Union as a state. Congress refused or never answered the request—no one is sure which. In 1841, El Salvador became an independent country.

Coffee Takes Over

The invention of artificial dyes almost ended the

indigo trade. In the 1840s the landowners began growing coffee. For coffee they needed even more land and more people to work it. So the government took away the land that the campesinos shared for growing vegetables and beans and gave the land to the rich. The campesinos could no longer even grow their own food. They had no choice but to work on the new coffee fincas for half a colon a day. Many Salvadorans believe that this action by the government more than 100 years ago was the root cause of the war in the 1980s.

Over the years there were several presidents who tried to give the campesinos more land, more rights, and more control over their lives. But when a president didn't do what the rich people wanted, he was overthrown by the military or assassinated. The military's role was to control the government, and the government's role was to keep the rich people rich.

La Matanza

In 1929 the Stock Exchange on Wall Street in the United States crashed, and the world economy collapsed. This collapse led to the Great Depression. In El Salvador many people lost their jobs. Wages on the fincas were cut to a quarter of a colon a day, and many campesinos were starving. President Arturo Araujo wanted to take some land away from the rich and give it to the campesinos. The military overthrew Araujo and replaced him with Maximiliano Hérnandez Martínez, who was called El Brujo ("The Witch") behind his back. When Martínez took power, people knew that the situation wouldn't get better.

In 1932, people all over the country rebelled against the government. Their leader was a man named Augustín Farabundo Martí, the leader of the Salvadoran Communist Party. Martí was quickly captured and executed. Then the government army began killing people who were involved in the rebellion. Soon they began killing anybody who looked like a Pipíl. Within a week the military had killed about 30,000 people. Because of this incident, called La Matanza or "The Slaughter," people became afraid to wear traditional Pipíl clothing or speak the Nahuatlan or Pipíl languages. The Pipíl culture began to disappear.

The Catholic Church supported President Martínez because he was against communism. The priests even gave prayers of thanks for La Matanza. For more than 400 years, the Church had supported the wealthy and the military in El Salvador. But soon the Church would change sides.

Times of Change

During the 1950s and 1960s, things seemed to get a little better. The government permitted the organization of a few labor unions and passed laws fixing a minimum wage and establishing a social security system. But the government was still controlled by the rich, and an organization called Orden ("order") was created to attack people who disagreed with the government. The people voted for the president, but often there was only one candidate. If there were two candidates, the election results were sometimes rigged so that the rich people's candidate would win. Most people still worked on land belonging to the wealthy and were paid very little.

By the 1970s many believed that labor unions and elections would not solve their problems. In the Church, people began talking about the ideas of liberation theologists and formed Christian Base Communities to work on solutions to El Salvador's problems. Other people joined rebel groups. Meanwhile, the government was becoming more repressive. People who disagreed with the government were beaten or killed, or they just disappeared.

El Salvador at War

In February 1977, Monsignor Oscar Arnulfo Romero was appointed archbishop of El Salvador. Romero seemed to be on the side of the government and the rich. But when a priest who disagreed with the government was murdered, Romero changed. In weekly radio sermons that were played on loudspeakers in the village plazas, he told the people that they had the right to rebel against a government that abused them. People called him "the voice of the voiceless."

That same year the military arranged the votes in the presidential election to elect Carlos Humberto Romero, no relation to the archbishop. President Romero had a plan he called "The Well-Being of Everybody." But soon 300 people who were protesting his election were shot in San Salvador. There were more murders and more disappearances than before. Death squads tracked down and killed people who were suspected of being against the government.

The violence and injustice were getting worse, and the Salvadoran people were becoming very angry. The campesinos were demanding land, and the factory workers were demanding higher wages. As more Salvadorans disappeared or were killed, more people joined the rebels. More Church members, priests, and nuns joined the liberation theologists.

In 1979, a group of military officers overthrew President Romero and promised to get rid of the death squads, introduce reforms, and raise people's wages. But these officers were overthrown by other officers who in turn were overthrown by more officers, and the murders continued. Hundreds of campesinos were gunned down by the army while trying to cross the Sumpul River into

Archbishop Romero is a hero to many Salvadorans today.

Honduras. The army fired on protestors in the Plaza Barrios and killed dozens of them.

On March 23, 1980, Archbishop Romero gave his weekly sermon on the radio. He asked the soldiers to stop killing the Salvadoran people. He told them to obey God, not the orders of their officers. On the following day Romero was murdered while celebrating Mass at the Divine Providence Cancer Hospital. At his funeral in the Metropolitan Cathedral, army snipers attacked the crowd and killed about 60 people. Although El Salvador had seen several years of violence already, this event is considered the beginning of the civil war.

Different rebel groups joined together to form the FMLN, or Farabundo Martí National Liberation Front, named for the leader of the 1932 rebellion. Because the FMLN wanted to take land from the rich and give it to the poor, it was considered a Communist group. Some people in the United States thought that the FMLN was supported by the Soviet Union, a Communist country.

The United States Gets Involved

The United States Congress decided to take the side of El Salvador's military against the FMLN. Congress voted to send money to the Salvadoran government. Many people in the United States protested against this aid, because the Salvadoran government was hurting the Salvadoran people. Several U.S. citizens had also been killed by the Salvadoran government army or the death squads.

Ronald Reagan was elected President of the United States in 1980. Reagan was strongly against Communism. So were many members of Congress. But other members of Congress were concerned as more and more terrible stories came out of El Salvador. The United States government, therefore, developed a plan called "recertification." Every six months, the Salvadoran government had to prove that it was improving its human-rights policy and that fewer people were being murdered. If the government could do this, the United States Congress would keep sending money, as much as a million dollars a day.

But no matter what happened, Congress always gave El Salvador its "recertification." In January, 1982, reports of a terrible massacre by the government army in the village of El Mozote reached the United States. The United States government sent investigators to find out what had happened. But the Salvadoran government soldiers refused to take the investigators to the village. The investigators never reached El Mozote and as a result told the U.S. government that they saw "no evidence" of a massacre. Congress gave El Salvador its recertification again.

As the death squads and massacres continued, the U.S. government told the Salvadoran government that it needed to hold elections. The Salvadoran government held presidential elections in 1984, when José Napoleón Duarte was elected, and again in 1989, when Felix Alfredo Cristiani, was elected. But the elections didn't seem to make the situation any better.

The War Ends

It seemed as if the war would go on forever. The FMLN wasn't strong enough to overthrow a government supported by the United States, but the government didn't seem to be able to get rid of the FMLN either. In 1989, peace talks began, but the FMLN walked out of the talks after the government bombed a labor-union office. On November 11, 1989, the FMLN launched an attack on San Salvador.

On November 16, soldiers from the battalion that had committed the massacre at El Mozote were ordered to kill Father Ignacio Ellacuria, a priest who had worked to start peace talks. The soldiers went to the Archbishop Romero Center at the University of Central America in San Salvador in the middle of the night and murdered all six of the priests who lived there, their housekeeper, and the housekeeper's daughter.

By the next morning it seemed that the whole world was angry at El Salvador. Some of the priests were from Spain, and the European nations were very unhappy. Many people in the United States were unhappy that the U.S. government was supporting a government that kept murdering people. Pressure from all over the world forced the Salvadoran government to start peace talks with the FMLN again. But the talks went on for more than two years, and the war continued.

On January 16, 1992, the Peace Accords, providing for military and political reforms, were signed at Chapultepec Castle in Mexico. The war in El Salvador ended. The government agreed to reduce the size of the army and to

Members of the FMLN gather at a rally in 1992.

get rid of the battalions and security forces that had been responsible for so much of the killing. The FMLN was changed from a rebel force into a new political party.

The two sides also agreed that a Truth Commission appointed by the United Nations would conduct an investigation and report on what had really happened during the war. The Truth Commission asked more than 2,000 Salvadorans about what they had seen and done during the war.

On March 15, 1993, the Truth Commission reported its findings, stating that 75,000 people had died during the

The war greatly affected everyone in El Salvador.
Here is one child's drawing of the war.

war and that about 95 percent of them had been killed by the government. It named the people responsible for the murder of Archbishop Romero, the massacre at El Mozote, and many other killings. On March 20, the Salvadoran government issued a general pardon for everybody mentioned in the Truth Commission's report. Nine soldiers who had been arrested earlier for the Jesuit murders were even included in the pardon. Nobody would be held responsible for the crimes committed.

Today and Tomorrow

Is El Salvador at peace? The war is over. But during the war many guns were brought into El Salvador, and they are still there. Many former soldiers have become kidnappers or *ladrones* ("bandits"). Since the war's end, there have been between 8,000 and 9,000 murders a year in El Salvador. If the Truth Commission's report of deaths during the war is correct, this means that Salvadorans are in as much danger today as they were during the war.

In recent years El Salvador has had many official political parties. For several years after the war, the ARENA party, who represent the rich, remained in power, controlling the legislative assembly. President Cameron Sol, elected in 1994 to serve until 1999, is also an ARENA member. But in the 1997 elections for city mayors and the legislative assembly, two thirds of the candidates elected were from the FMLN and the other parties. Many of these candidates represented the campesinos, the liberation theologists, the workers, and the unemployed. Salvadorans hope that this change in the government will help to solve their country's problems.

Salvadorans feel that their country is no longer at war but not yet at peace. Although the elections have given people hope for a better future, the problems that caused the war have not been solved. The rich still own most of the land. Most Salvadorans do not make enough money to

These government offices display the symbol of the ruling ARENA party in 1996.

meet their families' basic needs. There are new problems, too. During the war more than a million people became refugees, 75,000 people died, and many thousands of people disappeared. Now those who survived must learn to live together in peace.

MONSTERS, JOKES, AND SAD STORIES

When people get together, they like to tell one another jokes and stories. Jokes in El Salvador are very much like jokes in the United States. Here is a Salvadoran joke.

A man went to a pet shop to buy a dog. The shopkeeper offered him a special deal. "For only 5,000 colons," he said, "you can have a dog that can read."

The man bought the dog and took it home, anxious to show off his new pet to his friends. "Look," he told them. "I have a dog that can read."

So his friends put a newspaper down in front of the dog. But the dog just sat there, looking at it. They brought him another newspaper and a magazine, but the dog just sat there, looking at them. The man was very annoyed and took the dog back to the pet shop.

"I want my 5,000 colons back!" he said. "You told me this dog could read."

The pet-shop owner brought a newspaper and put it in front of the dog. The dog just sat there, looking at it.

"You see?" said the man. "The dog can't read."

"Sure, he can," said the pet-shop owner. "I said he could read; I didn't say he could talk."

Spooks and Monsters

In the countryside most children hear stories from their grandmothers or other adults. Often the stories are about monsters and scary creatures that come out at night. They hear stories about La Ciguanaba, which means "river woman" in the Nahuatlan language. La Ciguanaba appears from a distance to be a beautiful woman who washes her hair in the river. But if someone comes too close, she raises her head and reveals a face so terrifying that one look at it will make a person crazy. When somebody seems to be stunned or shocked, Salvadorans say, "You look like you've seen La Ciguanaba."

Many children are afraid of El Cadejo, a monster that howls in the night. Sometimes people tell children that if they don't go to sleep when they're told to, El Cadejo will come and get them. Of course, thinking about monsters doesn't make it any easier for them to get to sleep!

A much sadder story is about a creature called La Llorona del Río, who lost her son in an earthquake in Guatemala in 1917. She has been looking for him in the mountains of Guatemala and El Salvador ever since. His name was Juan Cruz, and in the night her voice can be heard in the sound of the rivers, crying, "Cruz, Cruz, Cruz . . . ."

In the early 1990s, Salvadorans began telling stories about another creature, La Descarnada. She is a hitchhiker who stops drivers on country roads and asks for a ride. If a

Grandparents share stories with their grandchildren.

driver gives her a ride, she'll get into the car but won't say anything at all. But as soon as the driver speaks to her, the flesh will disappear from her body, and she will turn into a skeleton.

The newest subject of monster stories in El Salvador is the Chupacabra. Nobody has ever seen this monster, but it sucks the blood of goats and leaves them dead. People think that the Chupacabra might be a giant bat.

Most children find these stories frightening. Some adults believe that scary stories are bad for children and that it's better not to tell such stories. Many Salvadorans say that they don't really believe in spooks and monsters anyway and that the stories probably aren't true. But then, they say, who knows?

Sad Stories

Many of the stories that people tell one another in El Salvador are hundreds of years old. Usually the stories are told by grandparents, sitting under a tree or in the doorway of a house, to the young people of the family and their friends. Almost all of the stories have sad endings. If a story has a happy ending, people may be dissatisfied with it. "*La vida no es así,*" they say. "Life is not like that."

La Tatuana

Long ago, when people still knew the secrets of plants and the language of stones, there lived a teacher who knew more about these things than anybody else. He had the power of turning himself into an almond tree while he sent his soul to wander the highways and footpaths of El Salvador.

Once while he was a tree in the forest, sending forth pink

blossoms in the springtime, his soul wandered into the city, where a rich merchant tried to catch it. The merchant succeeded in grabbing a piece of it, but the rest of the soul escaped and ran back to the teacher to tell him what had happened.

The teacher immediately turned himself back into a man, with hair and beard as pink as almond blossoms, and went to the city to find the missing piece of his soul. In the marketplace he asked around until he found the merchant who had the piece of his soul, locked in a crystal box.

"I believe you have a piece of my soul in that box," said the teacher. "I need it back. How much are you asking for it?"

"It's not for sale," said the merchant.

"I'll give you a barrel of pearls for it," said the teacher.

"I would not even sell it for a barrel of emeralds," said the merchant.

"Then I will give you a lake of emeralds."

"I said it's not for sale."

"I will give you a magic charm that has the power to turn away storms and stop earthquakes."

"No," said the merchant. "It's worth more than that. On my next journey over the mountains, I intend to trade this piece of soul for the most beautiful slave in the slave market."

The teacher went away, heartbroken. With his soul incomplete he did not know what to do, and he wandered aimlessly through the streets of the city.

Soon the merchant went on a long journey to trade goods in the lands over the mountains. When he came to the country where slaves were sold, he traded the piece of the teacher's soul for the most beautiful slave in the slave market. As the merchant and the slave came down from the mountains and crossed the plain toward the merchant's city, a terrible storm came up. The sky grew dark as night, and there were blinding flashes of white lightning and deafening roars of thunder. The merchant's pack horses fled. The thunder grew louder and the earth shook. Then with a mighty crash a chasm opened in the earth beneath the merchant's feet, and in he fell. The earth closed over him, and he was seen no more.

When the storm was over, the relatives of the merchant found the slave and brought her to the city. The teacher was still wandering the streets of the city. He had become very strange, his pink hair and beard a tangle of weeds and sticks, his only companions a pack of wild dogs. He went from door to door, asking everybody, "Do you know what has become of the lost part of my soul?" Everyone he asked slammed the door in his face, and some of them even complained to the police.

One day he knocked on the door of the house where the slave lived. "Do you know what has become of the lost part of my soul?" he asked her.

"Yes," she said.

At that moment the police arrived and arrested them both because of what had happened to the merchant. The police accused the teacher and the slave of being witches, or perhaps possessed by demons. In those days these were the very worst of crimes, so the mad teacher with the pink hair and the beautiful slave were condemned to be burned at the stake in the plaza of the city.

The night before the execution, the teacher called on the few magical powers he had left. He took his fingernail and made a tattoo of a little boat on the arm of the slave.

"Now you are called La Tatuana, 'the tattooed one'," he said, because the slave had no name. "Close your eyes and trace this little boat with your finger, then climb into the boat, and you will be free. It will take you wherever you want to go. And if you, who were bought with part of my soul, go free, perhaps my soul will be whole again."

In the morning when the constables came to carry out the sentence of death, they found the jail empty except for a dried-up almond tree, with a single pink blossom still hanging from its branches.

El Cadejo

On dark, starless nights, everyone is a little afraid of El Cadejo, that fierce, formless beast of the night that captures souls. This is the story of how El Cadejo came to the world.

Long ago there was a holy woman named Sister Maria, who was known throughout El Salvador for her kindness, wisdom, and charity. But even longer ago, Sister Maria was a novice, a young girl in training to become a nun. Most of the novices worked in the orchards and gardens belonging to the church. But Maria was paralyzed. She couldn't move her legs. So her job was to cut up and count out the hosts, the holy bread used in the church ceremony of Holy Communion.

Even then people suspected that Maria had very special powers. Sitting in her small room, or cell, she seldom spoke, but when she did, her voice and words were so full of lovingkindness that those who heard her went on their way feeling as though they had been conversing with angels. Her words were what they remembered, not the rather plain, mousey-looking girl with the long black braid.

But what nobody knew was that at night, Maria wrestled with demons. Her dreams were full of slimy, fiery beasts that shrieked and wailed and spoke words full of anger and hatred. In the morning, Maria would look at the sunlight streaming into her cell and whisper, "It was only a dream." But she was never entirely sure it had been.

Of course, not everyone in those times and in that place was full of lovingkindness. And those with evil hearts seldom know goodness when they see it.

There was a merchant who, once a week, carried the holy bread to the villages that lay to the east. He didn't do the job for religious reasons, but because he had to make the trip anyway and because he was paid a little bit and mostly because he wanted to see Maria. He dreamed of kidnapping her and carrying her off to his little hut on the mountain and keeping her there as his slave. Because his heart was full of greed and selfish thoughts, he couldn't see Maria's goodness, and he mistook it for beauty.

Each time he arrived, he grew a little bolder, standing a little closer to Maria and staring a little harder. When he did, Maria sensed the beasts from her nightmares stirring in the corners of the cell.

One day he was standing as usual, watching Maria count out the hosts. Suddenly he sprang forward, knocking the pieces of holy bread to the ground and trampling them under his feet. He grabbed Maria around the waist. As soon as his hand brushed her braid, his mind was filled with images of horrible, slimy, cold beasts that seemed to crawl over his body, their dripping fangs hungering for his throat.

"It's the hair!" he cried, and seizing the machete that hung at his side, he slashed off her long black braid. It fell writhing on the floor—perhaps a serpent, or perhaps a fat, venomous lizard. The merchant turned to flee. But he never reached the door. The beast crept under his feet, encircled his legs, tripped him, and engulfed him in its cold, sour embrace. Before he could scream, the beast had lifted him and borne him to a place where selfish and evil thoughts and acts belong.

And Maria? She didn't see what happened. As soon as her braid was cut off, all her evil dreams left her. She fell into a trance, listening to the song of the angels.

Those who knew Maria in later life, when her acts of charity and kindness were spoken of all over Central America, were amazed to think that El Cadejo had grown from her head. And what is El Cadejo exactly? Some people who have seen it at a distance say that it is sort of like a snake, and sort of like a bat, but mostly like a giant, hairy dog. People who have seen it up close—well, those people are never heard from again.

FIESTAS

In El Salvador, fiestas, or holidays, are celebrated by the whole community. The entire town attends *desfiles*, or "parades," carnivals, dances, and athletic contests.

A Festival for Every Town

Many towns in El Salvador are named after saints, holy people of the Catholic Church. Catholics believe that the saints are in heaven and are able to help people on earth. Every town has a patron saint, looked upon as a special guardian of the town, who protects it from danger. Some large towns have several patron saints. Each town has a *fiesta patronal*, or "patron saint's festival," every year to honor its patron saint. Festivals may continue for days or weeks and include parties, traditional dancing, sporting events, plays, concerts, and a desfile. The festival celebrations are a mixture of European and traditional Pipíl customs.

People look forward to their town's festival all year long, and the preparations of food and drink for a festival can take two weeks or longer. During festivals in the smaller towns, most people don't go to work or school. Businesses shut down, and everybody concentrates on celebrating.

Young girls march in the Fair of Palms procession in Panchimalco.

But the desfile is a very serious part of every festival. A picture or statue of the town's patron saint is carried through the town, held high over people's heads. People may follow the saint's image, carrying candles or religious symbols. There is usually a religious ceremony after the procession.

In Acajutla the San Rafael festival in October has a special desfile over the water. Fishermen in boats carry the saint's image from the town's new dock to its old dock. Then there is a religious ceremony on the dock.

Other festival activities are less serious. Each town has its own traditions. Some festivals are like big track meets, with all kinds of athletic competitions. Others include dances and plays that have been performed in the same way for hundreds of years.

The town with the most festival days is San Vicente. The Romería del Señor de Esquipulas ("Pilgrimage of the Lord of Esquipulas") lasts all through January and includes desfiles and costumes. Nuestra Señora del Rosario ("Our Lady of the Rosary") and La Fería de los Santos ("the Fair of the Saints") last from the beginning of October until mid-November. The San Vicente festival lasts from the middle to the end of December. Then it's time to start over again with the Romería festival. Altogether three months of the year are taken up with festivals. During the other nine months, the people of San Vicente have to be satisfied with getting on a bus and going to festivals in other towns.

Traditional dances are an important part of many festivals.

Special Dances

Traditional dances, some dating from before the arrival of the Europeans, are an important part of every festival. Dancers perform in the streets, sometimes wearing special costumes to act out a play.

El Torito Pinto ("the little speckled bull") is a dance that comes from the Pipíl and is performed at many fiestas. Men dressed up as bulls, wearing painted papier-mâché bull heads, chase children, and other men with lassoes try to catch the bulls, while a band plays music.

The Baile de Los Historiantes ("dance of the historians") is a story-dance. Dancers act out scenes from the ancient history of Cuzcatlán. Some parts of the dance tell about the history of Spain.

Día de los Difuntos

November 2 is Día de los Difuntos, or "Day of the Dead" (also called All Souls' Day). It's a day when Salvadoran families get together and go to the cemetery to spend time remembering family members who have died. They clean their relatives' graves and decorate them with flowers.

People often take a picnic to the cemetery and spend the day eating and visiting with friends as well as tending graves. It is like having a big party in the cemetery. A lot of families go to the cemetery on November 1 instead because they say it is just too crowded on Día de los Difuntos.

La Virgen de Guadalupe

Many towns celebrate the festival of the Virgin of Guadalupe. In 1531 an image of the Virgin Mary with dark skin and Native American features appeared to a Native American named Juan Diego at Guadalupe, Mexico. The day of the appearance, December 12, is celebrated throughout Mexico and Central America. In many Salvadoran towns there is a parade, with musical bands, fireworks, and people dressed in traditional Pipíl clothing.

Christmas

The celebration of El Nacimiento del Niño Jesús ("the birth of the baby Jesus"), also called La Navidad, is changing in El Salvador. Traditionally, Christmas carols, dances, processions, and fireworks on Christmas Eve are followed by the Misa de Gallo, or "Rooster's Mass," at the church at midnight. Children go from house to house, singing. If the people in a house bring the children something to eat, they sing happy songs, but if they do not, the children sing sad songs. In San Vicente the children dress up as shepherds to go caroling. In many towns, images of the Virgin Mary and St. Joseph are carried from house to house, and people are asked to give money for the church.

The celebration of Christmas lasts for more than a week, beginning on December 24 and ending on December 31, New Year's Eve. There are lots of Christmas parties as well as parades. In the town of Sonsonate, a mayor-for-a-night is chosen on New Year's Eve. The mayor usually orders that everybody in town be "captured," pretending they are all under arrest. The people who are captured have to pay a fine, which goes to charity.

In the last few years, Salvadoran Christmas traditions have begun to disappear in some towns, and traditions from the United States have taken their place. Santa Claus and Christmas trees have become an important part of Christmas in El Salvador as Salvadorans living in the United States have shared American Christmas customs with relatives back home. Now American-style Christmas decorations are put up every year in houses all over El Salvador. Cotton balls are glued to Christmas trees to look like snow.

New Year's Day is a national holiday. Many Salvadorans spend it resting up after the Christmas celebrations. In some towns the week after New Year's Day is another festival, the celebration of Los Reyes Magos, the three "wise kings" who came to visit the baby Jesus.

Semana Santa

Semana Santa, or "Holy Week," is the week before Easter. For Christians, Holy Week is a time to remember the death and resurrection of Jesus. Catholics and other Christians believe that Jesus was nailed to a cross and died on a Friday, which is remembered on Good Friday, and returned to life on Sunday, which is celebrated on Easter Sunday.

In many towns there is a procession on Good Friday in which people carry a glass coffin. Some towns have a procession of crosses. People of the town walk the 14 Stations of the Cross posted in different parts of the town. The Stations represent 14 events of Jesus' final suffering and show him on his way to die on the cross. In Sonsonate a play about Jesus being captured and killed is acted out in the town.

A Holy Week procession in Sonsonate, El Salvador

In Texistepeque, the whole town takes part in a play. Seven people dressed as devils run around town, pretending to hit people with whips. A man dressed as Jesus appears. The devils surround him and try to beat him. He shows them a cross, and the devils fall to the ground.

Fiestas Agostinas

The biggest festival in El Salvador takes place in San Salvador during late July and early August. It's called the Fiesta del Salvador del Mundo, the "Festival of the Savior of the World," or the Fiestas Agostinas, "August Festivals," for short.

The festival begins with the election and coronation of a queen of the August Festivals. Then children's parties are held in the parks and marketplaces. Salvadorans enjoy band concerts and performances of traditional music and dances. There are a lot of parades, including the traditional Desfile del Correo, a parade of government workers.

Other parades feature antique carriages, floats, and bands. There is a big carnival, lasting ten days, with more than 100 rides and more than a dozen different circuses. Vendors sell *pupusas*, the Salvadoran national dish. Pupusas are thick tortillas with a cheese, meat, or vegetable stuffing. There are sporting events and a giant chess game in the Plaza Barrios.

The festival honors San Salvador's patron, El Salvador del Mundo, or "the Savior of the World," symbolized by a statue of Jesus on top of a globe that stands on a pedestal in the western part of the city. The festival includes many religious events and ends with a ceremony called the Bajada del Salvador del Mundo, the "Descent of the Savior of the World."

Independence Day

September 15 is Independence Day in El Salvador as well as in the other Central American countries and Mexico. In El Salvador the celebration lasts almost a week, from September 10 to September 15. It is especially important for schools. Students march in a parade in their uniforms. Each school's *banda de guerra*, a band with trumpets and drums, marches. There is a contest to choose the best band in the country.

Special Days

Many countries have a Mother's Day and a Father's Day, and so does El Salvador. But in El Salvador there is a day for almost everyone—Teacher's Day, Pastor's Day, Doctor's Day, Secretary's Day, Postal Worker's Day, and many others. On their special day, people who do the same kind of work often get together to have parties and celebrate. For Salvadorans whose job doesn't have its own day, there is Día del Trabajo, or "Day of Work," to celebrate. And there is also a Día del Niño, "Children's Day."

Piñatas

Most festivals and holidays are times for both adults and children to have parties. At the parties are music, dancing, eating, and often a piñata for children. A piñata is a big papier-mâché model of an animal or a comic-book character covered with colorful crepe paper. The piñata is filled with pieces of candy and is hung from the ceiling. Children take turns trying to hit it with a stick. The person who is hitting wears a blindfold. Eventually the piñata breaks, and the candy spills out. Then everybody runs to pick it up.

Real piñatas can be as big as six feet tall. They are not often seen in the United States. Salvadorans who live in the United States sometimes bring piñatas back from visits to El Salvador. Here are directions for making a simple piñata.

Materials

a balloon	newspaper
flour	crepe paper and glue
water	individually wrapped candies

Blow up the balloon and tie it. To make papier-mâché, mix a few tablespoons of flour with a cup of water to make a thick paste. Tear the newspaper into strips. Dip a strip into the paste and then run the strip between your fingers to remove the extra paste. The whole strip should be wet, but if you use too much paste, your piñata will not dry. Lay the strip on the balloon. Keep adding strips until the whole balloon is covered with three layers of strips. Leave a bare spot about an inch wide near the knot in the balloon.

Let the balloon dry on a newspaper. When the top is dry, turn the balloon over so that the bottom doesn't stay wet. It may take a day or two to dry completely.

When the piñata is dry, pop the balloon with a pin. Decorate the piñata by gluing colored crepe paper on it or painting it with poster paints. When the paint or glue is dry, put the candy inside.

To hang the piñata, poke two holes at the top, each about an inch away from the bigger hole. Run a string through the holes. When you hang the piñata, make sure to tie it tightly.

Now you're ready to take turns trying to hit the piñata. A broom handle makes a good stick. Everybody should stand far away from the person who's swinging the stick. Remember, the person who is hitting needs to wear a blindfold.

SALVADORANS AT HOME

While crossing the city of San Salvador on a bus, a person will pass many different kinds of houses. There are mansions on the hillsides, apartment buildings and row houses in downtown neighborhoods, and houses—made of anything people can find—in the ravines. Inside the homes are small families or extended families, which may include parents, grandparents, aunts, uncles, and cousins living together and sharing what they have.

In the countryside there are small houses and larger ones occupied by large families or by several families together. Houses are made of *baharaque* (a mixture of mud, sticks, and sugar-cane stalks), adobe, logs, or concrete. Often doors are made of steel, and windows are barred to protect the family against thieves. Roofs are made of corrugated tin, shaped in wavy ridges, or *tejas*, curved clay tiles. Over the front doors of all kinds of houses, in the country and the city, there is often an aloe plant in a pot. Many Salvadorans believe that such a plant over the door brings good luck.

A Big Family Home

The Anónimo family lives in a long concrete house that

Houses in Panchimalco

grew bigger as the family grew. Before the civil war Señora Anónimo shared the house with her grown children, their wives and husbands, and their children. Each time a family member married, another room was added to the back of the house. Now a long line of rooms stretches back from the original one-room house on the village street.

Each room has a steel door opening onto a covered walkway. The walkway has a dirt floor and a tin roof, but no outside wall. Family members can step from the walkway right out into the courtyard, where there is a *lavadero* (a stone table with a sink in the middle of it for washing clothes), a clothesline, and a garden of tomato and pepper plants and rosebushes. Next to the courtyard is the living room, which has a roof and only three walls. The fourth side opens onto the courtyard. The family can sit comfortably on the couch and enjoy the outdoors, even when it's raining.

On the other side of the courtyard is the kitchen, where there is a hand mill with a crank for grinding corn and a fireplace with a griddle for cooking tortillas. There is a huge, dome-shaped clay oven that also burns wood. Like most families in El Salvador, the Anónimos use wood for cooking. However, wood is scarce and is sometimes more expensive than electricity. The Anónimos buy their wood from a man who collects fallen branches and sells them door to door.

At the back of the house is an outhouse, a room for bathing, and a yard where several chickens and a rooster live. Because the walkway has a dirt floor, the tile floors in the rooms get dirty. The Anónimo women mop the floors several times a day.

The Anónimo home has running water, but it is available for only an hour or two every few days. To get enough water for mopping, bathing, and cooking, the family has designed a system of gutters that carry rain from the roof to barrels all over the house. There are barrels in the kitchen, the courtyard, and outside the bathing room.

Wood fires are used for cooking and to heat water for washing.

When it rains, the water gushes along the gutters into the barrels. As soon as one barrel fills, the gutters can be moved around to fill another barrel. During invierno when it rains a lot, nobody has to carry heavy buckets of water from the public faucet. The gutters do all the work.

If family members want to take a bath, they can just get a bucketful of water from the barrel near the bathing room and take it inside. They can pour water over themselves, wash with soap, and then pour more water over themselves until all the soap is gone. During hot weather a bucketful of cool water feels very pleasant. But during invierno it's better to heat the water over the kitchen fire first.

To wash clothes, the Anónimos fill the stone sink with water from the barrel in the courtyard. Then they fill a basin with water from the sink. After soaking the clothes in the basin, they rub them with a thick cylinder of laundry detergent and then scrub them against the stone table of the lavadero. After thorough rinsing with more water, the clothes are even cleaner than they would be if they had been washed in a washing machine.

Electricity lights all of the rooms in the house and runs a refrigerator and a television set. The Anónimos especially enjoy a movie channel from nearby Guatemala that broadcasts American movies dubbed in Spanish. Relatives and friends come over in the evening to watch movies with them.

When friends come in the afternoon, they often sit in the

front room, drink a cup of coffee, and talk. The family always welcomes visitors with *"Pasen adelante!"* ("Come on in!") But if visitors stay too long, it is difficult to ask them to leave. Some Salvadorans believe that a guest who has stayed too long will leave if a broom is placed next to the door. Sometimes this strategy works—sometimes it doesn't!

An Empty Room

Before the recent civil war, 20 people lived in Señora Anónimo's house. Today only Señora Anónimo, her daughter, her daughter's husband, and their three children remain. Two family members were killed in the war. Several others disappeared. Two couples went to the United States with their children. The house is much quieter than it used to be and less busy. Once several people slept in each room in rows of beds, but now there is extra space and even an empty room.

Many Salvadoran families lost members during the war. Many were killed, and many more went to the United States. Others disappeared and were never found. In families where a member disappeared, the mourning continues. Family members know their relative is probably dead, but they still expect him or her to knock on the door at any moment.

Most of the dead and missing and those who left the country are men. Many husbands and fathers are gone.

Today most children in El Salvador live with one parent, usually their mother. These parents often have a double job to do, taking care of the home and the children and going out to earn a living.

Women's Work

In downtown San Salvador and out in the countryside, it is common to see women carrying things on their heads—basins of dried corn, baskets of fruit, tall plastic jugs of water, or bundles of firewood. To balance the load and make it more comfortable, the woman twists a towel, coils it into a circle, and places it on the top of her head. When men carry heavy loads, they tend to carry them under their arms or balance them on their shoulders. But most of the time, women are doing the carrying.

In most families, women's traditional work includes carrying water and firewood, washing clothes, grinding corn, making tortillas, cooking, making and mending clothes, cleaning the house, and taking care of the children. Women who are raising their children alone usually need their children to help them more in the home. They expect their children, especially their daughters, to help with getting water and wood and doing the laundry. If the women are very busy, they may buy tortillas and other food instead of making meals from scratch.

A woman carries a basin on her head in San Salvador.

Men traditionally repair things that break in the house and work for money on the coffee fincas or at other jobs. These are important jobs, too, but they don't take as much time as women's jobs do. On Sundays, village and city streets are full of men visiting with their friends, but most women are at home, working.

Some Salvadorans think that women should do more work than men because they are not as important as men. This sense of masculine pride is called machismo. Other people believe that men and women are equally important but have different jobs to do. They each do their jobs because they share the responsibility of caring for their families.

Now that many women are doing both their own work
and men's work, they are facing extra difficulties. Just as
in most other countries, it is harder for women to find jobs
than for men. When women in El Salvador do find jobs,
they are usually paid less than men. Many women are
forming labor unions and joining women's rights organizations to work on solving these problems.

Many women joined the FMLN and fought in the war.
When the war ended, some were eager to go home and
take care of their families. Others did not want to go back
to the way things used to be. After risking their lives for
years to try to make things better in El Salvador, they wanted to work on making things better for women. Today El
Salvador has many women's rights organizations that are
working to improve conditions for women in the work-
place, to obtain more legal rights for women, and to
prevent violence against women.

Making Tortillas

Salvadoran tortillas are much thicker and smaller than
the tortillas usually eaten in the United States. A stack of
tortillas is on the table at every meal.

Many families still use a *piedra de moler* and a *piedra
de mano* (grindstone and handstone) to grind *maíz*, or
"corn," by hand. The Anónimo family has a hand mill. The

A woman makes tortillas for her family.

women pour the corn into the top of the mill, turn the crank, and catch the cornmeal in a basin. They mix a little lime and water from the rain barrel into the basin and leave it to soak for a while. Then they wash their hands, wash the grindstone, and use it to mix the cornmeal into a thick dough. When the dough is mixed, they light a wood fire under the big iron griddle. Then they make the tortillas. First they dip their hands into water to keep them from sticking to the dough. They form a handful of dough into a ball. Then, by turning and patting the dough and smoothing the edges with their fingers, they quickly form it into a perfectly round tortilla.

It takes lots of practice to learn to make the dough round and flat. It's important to work quickly because the fire is burning all the time, and wood is expensive. The women lay a tortilla on the griddle, where it cooks for a minute or two. Then they turn the tortilla over to cook the other side. As each tortilla is finished, they pick it up with a spatula and add it to a stack of tortillas wrapped in a big cloth napkin. The napkin will keep the tortillas warm until it's time to eat them.

As soon as the tortillas are done, the women pull the sticks of firewood out of the fire and knock them against the floor to stop them from burning any more. It's important not to waste firewood.

A Salvadoran Meal

A good Salvadoran meal includes rice and salad as well as tortillas. Here is a simple dinner that you can make: *huevos rancheros* ("rancher-style eggs") with *arroz* ("rice") and *ensalada* ("salad"). A cup of hot milk with instant coffee and sugar stirred in or a *gaseosa* ("soda") is often drunk with dinner. If you have a Salvadoran friend who can show you how to make tortillas, that will make the meal complete.

Huevos Rancheros

Sauce
one tomato
one green pepper
one onion
1/4 cup olive oil
1/4 teaspoon salt
1/4 teaspoon ground cumin
1/4 teaspoon black pepper
1 teaspoon chili powder

Slice the tomato, green pepper, and onion into thin wedges. Pour the olive oil into a frying pan and place over low heat. Add the onions and peppers and fry them, stirring often, until they are soft. Add the tomatoes and the salt, cumin, black pepper, and chili powder. Cook for five more minutes, stirring often.

Eggs
2 tablespoons butter
2 eggs for each person

Topping
grated cheese

Melt the butter in a frying pan. Break the eggs into the pan. Be careful not to break the yolks. Cook the eggs over low heat until the clear part turns white. Then turn the eggs over. Cook them for 30 more seconds or until the white is set. Serve with the sauce poured over the eggs and a little grated cheese on top.

Arroz

1 cup rice	1 onion
2 cups water	1/4 teaspoon cumin
1 tomato	1/2 teaspoon salt
1/2 green pepper	1/8 teaspoon red pepper

Put the water and the rice into a pot. Chop the tomato, green pepper, and onion into small pieces. Put them on top of the rice. Add the cumin, salt, and red pepper. Cook, without stirring, over medium heat until the water boils. Then turn the heat down and cover the pot. Cook over low heat until all the water is absorbed. Stir well before serving. Serves four.

Ensalada

lettuce	lime
tomato	cucumber

Slice the cucumber and tomato thinly. Cut the lime into wedges. Put a few pieces of lettuce on each person's plate. Top with slices of tomato and cucumber. Give each person a wedge of lime to squeeze over his or her salad.

Chocobananas

one banana for every two people
two ice-cream sticks for every banana
1/3 cup milk
one tablespoon cocoa powder
one cup sugar
1/4 teaspoon salt

Cut each banana in half crosswise and insert an ice-cream stick into each half. Put the bananas into the freezer on a cookie sheet for an hour. Then mix the milk, cocoa, sugar, and salt together in a pot. Cook over medium heat and stir frequently with a wooden spoon. Boil the mixture until it reaches the soft-ball stage. To tell when it has reached the soft-ball stage, let a drop fall from the spoon into a bowl of cold water. If the drop falls apart or forms a ring, it's not ready. When the drop stays together in a soft ball at the bottom of the bowl, it's ready.

Let the mixture cool until it stops bubbling. Take the bananas out of the freezer. Dip each banana into the chocolate mixture and spoon chocolate over it until it is completely coated. Lay the bananas on waxed paper or a buttered plate. They will be cool enough to eat in about a minute, or you can put them back into the freezer and eat them later.

EVERYBODY WANTS TO STUDY

If asked how long they want to go to school, most Salvadoran students answer, "As long as I can." Sometimes it isn't easy to stay in school if a student's family needs him or her to work or can't afford to pay the bus fare. Most Salvadoran children get an elementary school education, but anything more than that may be difficult for the family to manage.

All over El Salvador *escuelas*, "public schools," meet twice a day. One group of students comes in the morning and a second group in the afternoon. In the cities some escuelas offer evening classes too so that children who work during the day have a chance to attend school. Some small towns don't have an escuela, so the children have to walk or ride a bus for a long distance to go to school. Parents who worry about sending small children to school alone sometimes keep their children out of school until they're old enough to make the long trip alone. That's why it's common to see children starting first grade at 10 or 11 years old, and children in third grade who are already teenagers.

A fifth-grade class in a rural school

Inside a School

Most schools have classrooms that open to the outdoors. In the countryside the classrooms often surround a big schoolyard with enough space to play basketball, softball, and soccer. Water spigots in the schoolyard provide drinking water. Sometimes there is a small shop where students can buy snacks and school supplies.

The classrooms are very open and airy, with big windows and high ceilings. The roofs are made of tin, and during invierno, when there are storms, the rain on the roof is so loud that it's hard to hear a word anybody says. The walls are covered with posters and maps that the teachers and students have made. Desks are arranged in rows or groups, with two students sitting at each desk. Usually students are allowed to talk to their deskmates and help one another with their work, as long as they aren't taking a test.

At most schools the students wear uniforms. Girls wear white shirts with blue or plaid skirts or jumpers. Boys wear white shirts and blue pants. Until recently many schools did not allow students to enter the classroom unless their uniforms were clean and pressed. Students were lined up for inspection, and those with dirty shoes, messy hair, or mismatched or wrinkled uniforms were sent home. But these strict rules are changing. People are beginning to feel that it is more important for children to be inside the classroom than to be dressed exactly alike.

Escuelas and Colegios

The school year in El Salvador begins in January and ends in October. Students have to be at least seven years old in January to start first grade, although many first graders are much older. Younger children can go to *kinder*, or kindergarten. Students can attend one or more years of kinder while they are waiting to be old enough for first grade.

Escuelas are free, except for an enrollment fee of 15 colons, and offer education through the ninth grade. A ninth-grade education is called *plan básico*. Students who want a *bachillerato*, or high school diploma, must attend a *colegio*, which is a private school and can be quite expensive. Three months of colegio costs about 425 colons.

In the escuela, students work very hard. Because each group of students comes to school for only four hours, no time is wasted. The pace is often much more intense than it is in schools in the United States. Students have to learn a great deal of information, do a lot of homework, and take frequent exams. Most classrooms don't have textbooks, so the teacher writes information on the chalkboard, which the students copy into notebooks to take home and study. Sometimes the teacher draws pictures on the chalkboard, and the students copy the pictures, too. Since there is so much hard work, many schools have an outdoor recess after every class period.

In the colegio the students are usually preparing for a career. If they want to be doctors, nurses, or health-care workers, they study at a colegio that offers a *bachillerato de salud*, or diploma in health. Afterward they can study at a college or university to get a medical or a nursing degree. If they want to be secretaries, teachers, or engineers, they

A collegio in San Salvador

take a different program and get a different bachillerato. Many colegios offer night classes. The students work during the day so that they can afford to attend school at night.

A Day at School

Maria is a student in a rural school in El Salvador. She goes to school in the morning. After breakfast she irons her school uniform, puts it on, and leaves the house at 7:30. She takes her bookbag to carry the 12 different notebooks she needs for her classes. On the way to school, she stops at a shop to buy a sheet of paper for 20 centavos (about 2 1/2 cents). If the teacher assigns any classwork to be handed in, she will do it on the sheet of paper. She goes into the schoolyard and crosses the playground to the fifth-grade classroom. The teacher asks her to help sweep out the room.

The teacher has written a paragraph on the board about mammals, reptiles, and amphibians. All of the students take out notebooks and copy the paragraph. The teacher tells the students to write down two examples of each kind of animal on the paper brought for classwork. When students have finished, they may go outside to play.

During recess the boys play soccer and the girls jump rope, and both girls and boys play softball. After 20 minutes a bell rings, and it's time to get back to work.

The teacher reads aloud some geometry problems for students to do on their classwork paper. Then they copy diagrams that the teacher draws on the board into their geometry notebooks. When they're finished, they may go outside again. Some students line up to buy bags of watermelon slices from a vendor at the gate and share them with their friends.

In language arts class the teacher gives back a spelling test and tells the students to copy each word that they missed ten times in their notebooks. Maria missed only two

Girls jump rope during recess in a rural school.

words, *magnánimo* ("magnanimous") and *maligno* ("malignant"). Then there is a vocabulary test. After the test, students exchange papers and grade them. The teacher writes another list of words on the board for the class to learn for tomorrow.

After another recess comes the last class of the day, social science. Today it will be fun because the class has formed groups to make maps of the world. Maria's group is making a topographical map, which shows the world's mountain ranges. When the bells rings, some of the students stay in the schoolyard to play softball and soccer. But Maria has to go home for lunch. After lunch she will get started on her homework, study her spelling and vocabulary words for tomorrow, and meet with her group to work on her topographical map. Then she might play softball with her friends.

Todos Quieren a Estudiar

Many Salvadoran children feel that studying is their most important job. "Todos quieren a estudiar," says a third-grader. "Everybody wants to study." But she goes on to say, "Not everybody can."

Her aunt disagrees. "A lot of people think education is only for the rich, so they never send their children to school. They make their middle children take care of their little ones and send their older children off to work in the fincas. And then the older children get married and start having children, and there's never any time for education. What kind of life is that?"

Many Salvadorans do get married very young and fail to finish their education. Some never get to go to school at all. But because the school day is very busy and so much time is spent studying new information, many Salvadorans learn a great deal in only a few years of schooling.

Problems for Teachers

Nowadays, somebody wanting to become a teacher must finish his or her bachillerato and then go to the university. But during the war many teachers were killed by the death squads because they belonged to a teacher's union. To replace the teachers, the government announced that anyone who had completed ninth grade could attend Escuela Normal, or teacher-training school, for six months and become a teacher. Recently the government closed the Escuela Normal to make another military base. But El Salvador now has many teachers who don't have a high school education.

There is still a shortage of teachers in El Salvador. In many schools, classes have 80 students or more. The teachers teach one huge group of students in the morning and another in the afternoon. Teachers are also expected to clean the school and often buy or make their own materials. No textbooks are supplied—students must buy their own books or do without. Some teachers feel that the government doesn't do enough to help the schools. They say the government is always telling them, *"Hagalo usted"* ("Do it yourself").

The government has many other problems to deal with, and it sometimes seems that money for education comes last. Teachers are paid about $1.50 an hour. In 1996 the government decided to close down five escuelas and turn the buildings into detention centers for juvenile delinquents. There is no money for repairing, painting, or cleaning schools or for buying supplies for students and teachers. One teacher says that the only thing the government supplies to teachers is chalk.

But the government's Ministry of Education also sponsors the Casas de la Cultura, which have brought libraries and cultural classes to many parts of the country, and the Parque Infantil in San Salvador, where children can learn about the environment as well as play. Recently the government announced that it will supply some textbooks for first- and second-grade classes. The Ministry is working on designing a special education system for children with special needs and on other new programs to update the country's school system.

Universities

El Salvador's two main universities are in San Salvador. They are the public National University, also called the University of El Salvador, and a university run by the Catholic Church, which is called the José Simeón Cañas University of Central America, or UCA for short. The National University was attacked by the government army during the civil war. Many students were killed, and the military stole the university's books and equipment and sold them. The university was closed down. Dozens of private universities opened in San Salvador where students paid a high tuition to complete their studies. Today the National University has reopened, but the private universities also remain open. In 1996 the government announced that many of these universities were granting "illegal" degrees—degrees that were not approved by the Ministry of Education. Thousands of students were told that the degrees they had earned were worthless.

The UCA remained open throughout the war. There were bombings and murders on the campus. Many of the students and teachers at the UCA were liberation theologists, so the military attacked them. Many professors quit because the military threatened to kill them. The murder of the six Jesuit priests, their housekeeper, and her daughter on November 16, 1989, happened on the UCA campus.

The military also has its own college. Students who want to be military officers can attend the Captain General Gerardo Barrios Military School. At the school the students learn to be loyal to the military and to their *tanda*, or "graduating class." Officers who are in the same tanda help members of the group throughout their careers by giving one another promotions and protecting one another. It is partly because of the tanda system that many members of the government's army were never held responsible for the murders they committed during the war. Some of the officers who graduated from the school joined the FMLN, the rebel army.

In many Salvadoran homes, bachilleratos and university degrees hang in picture frames on the living-room wall. The education of a family member is considered one of a family's greatest accomplishments. Education costs money, and it also takes time that could be spent earning money. Paying for an education may mean that a family lives in a smaller house and has less money for food and clothing. When people talk about getting an education, they often use the word *sacrificio*, ("sacrifice"). After a family makes these sacrifices to educate a son or daughter, he or she may then take responsibility for paying for the education of younger brothers and sisters.

FÚTBOL AND OTHER RECREATION

For Salvadorans of all ages, the most important sport is *fútbol*, or soccer. Escuelas and colegios have soccer teams. Universities have soccer teams. Villages and towns have their own teams, which play each other on Sundays, and soccer matches are often part of a town's festival. Children play soccer at playgrounds and on streets in residential neighborhoods. The best soccer players in the country are chosen for the *selección nacional*, the "national team." The national team plays against teams from other countries in international competitions.

Because El Salvador is a tiny country with a small population, it is difficult to compete with big countries like Brazil and Italy. Bigger countries have more people to choose from when they make up national teams, so they usually win international competitions such as the Olympics and the World Cup. But 1996 was a special year for fútbol in El Salvador. The El Salvador children's national team defeated teams from many bigger countries to win the children's World Championship in soccer.

The El Salvador National Amputees Soccer Team plays in the Boeing World Cup for soccer players with physical disabilities. The El Salvador team has won the

A Sunday afternoon soccer game in the village of Los Naranjos

worldwide competition several times.

Although no other sport is quite as popular as soccer, Salvadoran schools and towns also have baseball, softball, volleyball, and basketball teams for boys and girls as well as adults. Most large towns and cities have basketball courts, and people gather to play pickup games with anybody else who wants to play.

Sports Festivals

Sports competitions are an important part of many

patron saints' festivals and other festivals. Bicycle races, foot races, swimming competitions, and basketball tournaments are sometimes part of a town's festival. Most important of all, of course, are the soccer matches.

In Ahuachapán the Dulce Nombre de Jesús ("Sweet Name of Jesus") festival is celebrated with marathons— foot races of 26 miles 385 yards (42.2 kilometers), a motocross competition, swimming and bicycle races, and ping-pong, basketball, and soccer tournaments. The town of Panchimalco, near San Salvador, also features a marathon as part of its festival. In San Miguel the festival of Nuestra Señora de la Paz ("Our Lady of Peace") is celebrated with bicycle and motorcycle races as well as go-kart and hot-air balloon races.

Other Kinds of Recreation

El Salvador has miles of beaches whose volcanic black sands are crowded with families on weekends. Salvadorans like to go to the beach at La Libertad and swim. Los Chorros is a shady park where waterfalls fill several large natural rock-enclosed swimming pools. It doesn't cost very much to take a bus from San Salvador to these popular swimming spots. Wealthy people enjoy boating, water-skiing, and surfing at the beaches.

Hiking and mountain climbing are also popular forms

A stepping-stone bridge crosses a swimming pool at Los Chorros.

of recreation. A trip to the Montecristo Cloud Forest or to one of the other national parks may be too expensive for most Salvadorans, but there are plenty of volcanoes and other mountains that people can climb to find a beautiful view. People in the countryside enjoy climbing the mountains and spending a night sleeping under the stars. The San Salvador Volcano is a popular weekend climb for people in San Salvador.

Children's Games

Salvadoran children are clever at inventing games and making toys out of almost anything. A packing crate makes a good wagon for pulling one another around. Any kind of rope or string makes a good jump-rope. When children really use their imagination, just about anything they find can be turned into a new game.

The game hawk and rabbits is played outdoors. Children draw a big circle on the ground. One person is outside the circle. That person is the *gavilán*, the "hawk." Everyone inside the circle is a *conejo*, a "rabbit." The rabbits stand in a line, one behind another, and hold on to each other by the waist. The hawk tries to catch the last rabbit in the line. Every rabbit he catches is "out" and has to leave the circle. The rabbit in front has to protect the other rabbits by waving her arms. She tries to remain facing the hawk wherever he goes, and the other rabbits try to stay behind her. The hawk can come into the circle, but if the "head" rabbit touches the hawk, he has to leave the circle, and all of the rabbits that he has captured get to come back into the game. The hawk has to try to catch all of the rabbits within a certain period of time.

It takes four people to play the game straws. Players need an egg carton, two plates, and four straws. They also must tear up some paper into little pieces and put a few pieces of paper into each cup of the egg carton.

There are two teams of two people each. One person on each team has to pick up the bits of paper with one end of the straw while keeping the other end in her mouth. To do this, she has to pull in air through the straw. The players can't use their hands at all. Then the player passes the paper to a teammate. This teammate has to take the paper onto his straw by pulling in air through the straw and then let the paper fall onto his team's plate. If a team drops a piece of paper, that paper is out of the game and doesn't count. The team that has the most papers on its plate when the egg carton is empty wins.

To make the game harder, players can try to make the other team laugh by making faces at them while they play. If they laugh, of course, they will breathe out and drop their paper. But players often laugh without antics from the opposing team.

Marbles is also a popular game. To play one Salvadoran version of marbles, players find a box and cut five holes of different sizes in the side, very close to the bottom. The box sits on the floor. Players take turns rolling their marbles into the holes. The biggest hole is worth one point, the next biggest is worth two, and so on. The smallest hole is worth five points. If a player gets one point, the player to the right has to give him or her one marble. If a player gets two points, the player to the right has to give him or her two marbles, and so on. If there is no player on the right, then the player at the opposite end of the line has to give the active player the required number of marbles. The game ends when one player has all the marbles.

People play this game with as many marbles as they have. If players don't have marbles, they can play this game by rolling coins. A Salvadoran five-centavo coin, which is worth about half a U.S. cent, is a tiny coin that is good for games. Pennies can also be used. Of course, coins are much harder to roll than marbles are.

Children in El Salvador like to play *mica,* or "tag." There are many different kinds of tag. To play ring tag, children stand in a circle and hold hands tightly. One player is in the center of the ring and must try to get out by going under or over the children's hands. The children can move their hands up or down to try to block the player from getting out, but they can't use their feet. If the child in the center gets out, the two who let him through chase him and try to catch him. The one who catches him then goes into the center of the ring.

Another kind of tag is *mica encadenada*, or "chain tag." One person is "it." When she catches somebody, the two hold hands, and then they both try to catch the other players. As soon as somebody is caught, he joins hands with the player at the end of the chain. The game goes on until all of the players are part of the chain. The last one to get caught is "it" next time. If a lot of people are playing, the rules can be changed a little. Every time a chain has four people in it, the chain breaks into two chains. So instead of one long chain being "it," there are several little chains that are all "it."

LOS HERMANOS LEJANOS

Good Friday is an important part of Semana Santa, or "Holy Week." The parade that begins after dark is solemn and quiet. Salvadoran men, women, and children hold candles and flashlights in their hands as they form a procession. The procession moves slowly down a city street that has been closed to traffic. At the center of the crowd, several men carry a glass coffin high over their heads, representing the crucified body of Jesus. As they walk, the Salvadorans softly chant a prayer. This procession is just like any other Salvadoran Good Friday ceremony—except that it takes place in Washington, D.C.

Nobody is sure how many Salvadorans live in the United States today, but the number is probably about one million. Since the whole population of El Salvador is less than six million, that means that most people in El Salvador have at least one relative in the United States. These relatives are called *los hermanos lejanos*, which means "the faraway brothers and sisters." But about half of these immigrants are also mothers and fathers whose children are still in El Salvador living with other relatives. The parents send money to El Salvador to support their families. Most of the Salvadorans in the United States arrived in the 1980s, during the civil war.

These female restaurant workers are part of a large Salvadoran community in Washington, D.C.

The largest number of Salvadorans in the United States, perhaps as many as half a million, lives in Los Angeles. Other large Salvadoran communities are in San Francisco, Chicago, New York, Washington, D.C., and cities in Texas. Smaller numbers of Salvadorans are living in other cities and small towns in all 50 states.

Because of the war more than one fourth of the Salvadoran population had to leave home. Many who did not feel safe in El Salvador fled to Honduras and from there to Mexico. From Mexico many moved on to the United States. Mexico and the United States did not give the Salvadorans permission to stay. The Salvadorans felt that they had to hide in these countries and try not to be discovered. If they were found, they could be sent back to El Salvador.

Economic Refugees

When people have to leave their country because they are in danger, other countries sometimes give them political asylum. This means that the government of the new country will protect the person from the government of the home country by letting the person live in the new country. Many Salvadorans who came to the United States had barely escaped from the death squads in El Salvador. Others had lost family members. So they asked the United States government for political asylum. They asked to stay in the United States because they were afraid to return to El Salvador.

But the United States government was giving a lot of money to the Salvadoran government. Many people in the U.S. government did not believe that the stories they heard about El Salvador were true. They believed that El Salvador had a democratic government with a good human-rights record. So the U.S. government decided that the Salvadorans did not need political asylum and that the Salvadorans would be safe if they returned to El Salvador.

The U.S. government also said that the Salvadorans were "economic refugees"—that is, the Salvadorans were not coming to the United States to escape from the death squads, but to get jobs and make money. In 1986 the U.S. government passed a law to make it harder for people from other countries to get jobs in the United States.

The Threat of Deportation

When immigrants are found living in the United States without the government's permission, they can be deported, or sent home. They have the right to a court hearing during which they tell their story to an immigration judge. The immigrants have to prove that they have the right to remain in the United States. If the judge decides to deport them, the immigrants have 30 days to leave the United States. If they are still in the United States after 30 days, the U.S. Immigration and Naturalization Service, or INS, puts the immigrants on a plane or bus to their native country.

Salvadorans who faced deportation often asked the immigration judge for political asylum. The answer was almost always no. As a result, Salvadorans felt that it was far safer to remain hidden in the United States without asking for political asylum and hope that the INS officials would not find them.

Many Americans were concerned about the dangers that these Salvadorans faced. They wanted to protect people who might be killed if they were sent back to El Salvador. Hundreds of years ago in Europe, a person who was hiding from a king or an army could run into a church and claim sanctuary. This meant that nobody could capture the person unless he or she left the church. Many people in the United States thought that the Salvadorans needed such sanctuary. More than 300 American churches and synagogues declared themselves sanctuaries and promised to try to protect Salvadorans who needed to stay in the United States. Some cities declared themselves sanctuaries, too.

The sanctuary workers hid many Salvadorans and even operated an escape system like that of the Underground Railroad, which helped African Americans escape from slavery in the nineteenth century. The underground railroad for Salvadorans helped some of them get into the United States. Sanctuary workers sometimes went to Mexico and brought Salvadorans back with them. When necessary, the underground railroad could take Salvadorans all the way to Canada. But many sanctuary workers were arrested, and the people they were trying to help were sent back to El Salvador.

Every year thousands of Salvadorans were caught and sent back to El Salvador, where many died. But most were not caught. They were able to remain in the United States.

Temporary Protected Status

Not everybody in the United States government wanted to send the Salvadorans back to El Salvador. Many members of Congress were very worried about what might happen to these Salvadorans. They wrote a letter to the U.S. State Department and the Attorney General, asking that the Salvadorans be allowed to stay. But the State Department refused. The Attorney General said that if the Salvadorans who were already in the United States were allowed to stay, more Salvadorans would come. In 1986 the government reached a compromise. Salvadorans who had been living in the United States before 1982 were given amnesty. That meant they could stay in the United States until the situation improved in El Salvador.

In 1990, Congress passed another law. This law provided that people who were in the United States because of problems in their own country could stay in the United States until their country became safe. They were granted Temporary Protected Status, or TPS. People did not have to go to court and prove that they were in danger in order to get TPS. Congress stated that Salvadorans could stay in the United States until the war ended.

Even though the war in El Salvador is over, many Salvadorans in the United States still feel that they cannot return home safely. For now the U.S. government is not forcing them to go. The Salvadoran government also does not want its citizens back right away. While they remain in the United States, they are sending a lot of money to relatives in El Salvador. But if they all returned to El Salvador at once, they would no longer be sending money, and they would probably not be able to find jobs. It could mean big problems for El Salvador.

Sending Money Home

The Salvadorans did not come to the United States just to get jobs and make money, but those who were able to stay did make money. Since most Salvadorans were willing to work very hard for low pay, their work was a big help to many people in the United States. Many business owners found that they could increase production and save money if they hired Salvadorans. And since the businesses could keep their costs down, they could charge their customers lower prices. While some people feared that the Salvadorans might take jobs away from U.S. workers, studies show that immigrants actually create more jobs than they take away.

The Salvadorans who came to the United States in the 1980s lived very cheaply, sometimes crowding 20 or more people into a one-bedroom apartment to save on rent. They saved their money and sent it home to relatives in El Salvador. Most were able to send their families more than

100 dollars a month to help them get by.

Today Salvadorans in the United States send over a billion dollars a year to relatives in El Salvador. That is more money than El Salvador makes from any of its exports. Coffee is no longer El Salvador's chief product. It is Salvadoran workers in the United States.

Some Salvadorans think that this practice could cause problems for El Salvador in the future. Salvadorans have always believed in working hard for a better life. Now that many Salvadorans are receiving gifts of money from relatives in the United States, people are worried that the next generation of Salvadorans may be less hard-working.

So far there are no signs of this kind of change. But there are other problems. Most of los hermanos lejanos are young men who have a better-than-average education. During their years in the United States, some have become less attached to their families in El Salvador. They write and call less often. If they can, they become legal residents of the United States. They make friends, marry, and have children. They stop sending money home. Gradually El Salvador is losing many of its young, educated citizens.

Of course, many Salvadorans long to go back home. For them, living far away from El Salvador is a sacrifice that they must make to help their families. They dream of saving up enough money to start a business in El Salvador. Meanwhile, working in the United States is one way they can help make things better in El Salvador.

Intipuca is a small city in eastern El Salvador. More than half of Intipuca's population has left El Salvador and now lives in the suburbs of Washington, D.C. The 15,000 Intipuqueños who live in the D.C. area have formed a close community. They own several businesses and have their own soccer league and band. They have also organized committees to oversee improvements in their home city. The committees have arranged to have a new school built in Intipuca and to have the streets paved.

Back home in Intipuca, residents receive about $100,000 a month from their relatives in the United States. They miss their relatives, of course, but they hear from them often. Five courier services, as well as the postal service, serve the town. Airlines offer special fares to Intipuqueños who want to come home for the holidays.

Casitas is a smaller town with more than half of its population now living in the United States. Although the people from Casitas are not as organized as the Intipuqueños, they too have been able to improve the lives of their families back home. Every house in Casitas has electricity and running water.

Other towns and villages, like Valle Nuevo and San Jorge, became ghost towns. Their entire populations moved to the United States.

Salvadorans in the United States miss the family members they have left behind. They send money home to help their relatives in El Salvador and travel back to visit often.

A Few Hours on a Plane

El Salvador is not far from the United States. Even though so many Salvadorans live in a different country from that of their families, they can travel back to visit often. It takes less than four hours to fly from Los Angeles, California, to El Salvador. There are many flights a day between El Salvador and the large cities of the United States. Flights in both directions are often full of

Salvadorans who live in the United States.

When the passengers leave the United States, they are loaded down with heavy luggage. They are taking gifts to their families in El Salvador—often expensive gifts like televisions and VCRs. When they come back, they are loaded down with luggage again. The things they are bringing back are not expensive, but they are very important. Often there are large, colorful piñatas. Some people bring cakes from a popular bakery in San Salvador. Sometimes people bring hammocks, and chairs made of iron rods and plastic string that they have bought in the Central Market in San Salvador. Nearly everybody brings a big carton of fried chicken from Pollo Campero, El Salvador's favorite fast-food restaurant chain. With all of these big, strangely shaped, confusing pieces of luggage, it sometimes takes a long time to get all of the people and things onto the plane. But the things that people are bringing back remind them that no matter where they go, they will always be Salvadoreños.

APPENDIX

Salvadoran Embassies and Consulates in the U.S. and Canada

U.S. Embassy and Consulates

Washington, D.C.

Embassy of El Salvador
2300 California Street N.W.
Washington, D.C. 20008
telephone: 202-265-9671
E-mail:70754.3125@compuserv.com

Consulate General of El Salvador
1424 16th Street N.W.
Washington, D.C. 20036
telephone: 202-331-4032
E-mail: 75424.2306@compuserv.com

Boston

Consulate General of El Salvador
222 3rd Street #1221
Cambridge, Massachusetts 02142
telephone: 617-577-9111
E-mail: 75063.162@compuserv.com

Chicago

Consulate General of El Salvador
104 South Michigan #707
Chicago, Illinois 60603
telephone: 312-332-1393
E-mail: 75063.102@compuserv.com

Dallas

Consulate General of El Salvador
1555 West Mockingbird Lane #216
Dallas, Texas 75235
telephone: 214-637-1018
E-mail: 75063.110@compuserv.com

Houston

Consulate General of El Salvador
6420 Hillcroft Avenue, Suite 100
Houston, Texas 77081
telephone: 713-270-6239
E-mail: 75063.104@compuserv.com

Los Angeles

Consulate General of El Salvador
3450 Wilshire Blvd. #250
Los Angeles, California 90010
telephone: 213-393-6134
E-mail: 75063.550@compuserv.com

Miami

Consulate General of El Salvador
300 Biscayne Blvd. Way, Suite 1020
Dupont Plaza Center
Miami, Florida 33131
telephone: 305-371-8850
E-mail: 75154.157@compuserv.com

New York

Consulate General of El Salvador
46 Park Avenue
New York, New York 10016
telephone: 212-889-3608
E-mail: 75063.61@compuserv.com

New Orleans

Consulate General of El Salvador
1136 World Trade Center
New Orleans, Louisiana 70130
telephone: 504-522-4266
E-mail: 75063.100@compuserv.com

San Francisco

Consulate General of El Salvador
870 Market Street, Suite 508
San Francisco, California 94102
telephone: 415-781-7924
E-mail: 75154.161@compuserv.com

Santa Ana

Consulate General of El Salvador
1212 North Broadway Ave., Suite 100
Edificio Orleans
Santa Ana, California 92701
telephone: 714-542-3250
E-mail: 75063.76@compuserv.com

Canadian Embassy and Consulates

Ottawa

Embassy of El Salvador and
Consulate General of El Salvador
209 Kent Street
Ottawa, Ontario K2P 1Z8
telephone: 613-238-2939
E-mail: 103234.607@compuserv.com

Montreal

Consulate General of El Salvador
1080 Beaver Hall Côté, Suite 1604
Montreal, Quebec H2Z 1S8
telephone: 514-861-6515
E-mail: 104633.1466@compuserv.com

Toronto

Consulate General of El Salvador
151 Bloor Street West, Suite 320
Toronto, Ontario M5S 1S4
telephone: 416-975-0812
E-mail: 103504.2104@compuserv.com

GLOSSARY

anónimo (ah NOH nee moh)—anonymous; not named

bachillerato (bah chee yair AH toh)—a high school diploma

campesinos (kahm pay SEE nohs)—country people, usually farm laborers, or city people who were originally from the country

cantón (kahn TOHN)—a rural division of a department

casa de la cultura (KAH sah day lah kool TOO rah)—house of culture; a public building for learning about traditional dances, music, and art, sometimes including a public library

Christian Base Communities—groups of liberation theologists who join together to bring about changes in society

ciudad (see yoo DAHD)—city

cloud forest—a moist, humid forest

colegio (koh LAY hee oh)—a high school or a private elementary school

communism—an economic and political system in which all property is owned by the state and the society is placed under the control of a single party

conejo (koh NAY hoh)—rabbit

cruz (kroos)—cross

cumbia (KOOM bee ah)—a music style

Dios le bendiga (DEE ohs lay ben DEE gah)—God bless you; a Salvadoran greeting

desfile (des FEE lay)—parade

encomienda (en kohm YEN dah)—a grant of land from the king and queen of Spain

escuela (es KWAY lah)—a public elementary school that goes through eighth grade

fiesta (fee ES tah)—festival; holiday; party

fútbol (FOOT bohl)—soccer

gavilán (gah vee LAHN)—hawk

Great Depression—the period that began in 1929 and lasted through the 1930s during which the world's economy was in poor condition. Many businesses went bankrupt and many people were unemployed.

hacienda (ah see EN dah)—in El Salvador, a large tract of land for growing coffee

los hermanos lejanos (lohs air MAHN ohs lay HAHN ohs)—the faraway brothers and sisters; refers to Salvadorans living in the United States

invierno (een vee AIR noh)—winter

labor union—a group of workers who band together to try to improve their working conditions

latifúndio (lah tee FOON dee oh)—a large tract of land for growing crops other than coffee

liberation theology—a movement started in the Catholic Church in Latin America to use the Church to help liberate, or free, people from oppression

macehualtín (mah say wahl TEEN)—the class of people who farmed the land in Pipíl society

machete (may SHAY tay)—a wide knife used for farm work

merengue (may RAYN gay)—a music and dance style

mica encadenada (MEE kah en kah day NAH dah)—chain tag; a kind of tag game

minifundio (mee nee FOON dee oh)—a small tract of land for growing food

Occidente (ahk see DAYN tay)—the West

Oriente (oh ree AYN tay)—the East

piedra de mano (PYAYD rah day MAH noh)—hand stone; used for grinding corn

piedra de moler (PYAYD rah day moh LAIR)—grindstone; used for grinding corn

political asylum—protection given by the government of one country to people from another country

refugee—a person who has had to leave his or her home because of war or disaster

salsa (SAHL sah)—sauce; a music and dance style

Salvadoreño (sahl vah dohr AYN yoh)—a person from El Salvador

Semana Santa (say MAH nah SAHN tah)—Holy Week, the week leading up to Easter Sunday

tanda (TAHN dah)—graduating class of the national military school

telenovela (tay lay noh VAY lah)—soap opera

tortilla (tohr TEE yah)—thin, round pancake made of ground corn

verano (vay RAH noh)—summer

SELECTED BIBLIOGRAPHY

Alegria, Claribel. *Woman of the River.* Pittsburgh, PA: University of Pittsburgh Press, 1989.

Alegria, Claribel, ed. and Darwin J. Flakoll, trans. *On the Front Line: Guerrilla Poems of El Salvador.* Willimantic, CT: Curbstone Press, 1989.

Argueta, Manlio. *Magic Dogs of the Volcanoes.* San Francisco: Children's Book Press, 1990.

Brauer, Jeff, and others. *On Your Own in El Salvador.* Charlottesville, VA: On Your Own Publications, 1995.

Cummins, Ronnie. *Children of the World: El Salvador.* Milwaukee, WI: Gareth Stevens Children's Books, 1990.

Foran, Eileen. *El Salvador Is My Home.* Milwaukee, WI: Gareth Stevens Children's Books, 1992.

Haverstock, Nathan A. *El Salvador in Pictures.* Minneapolis, MN: Lerner Publications, 1987.

Volcán: *Poems from Central America.* San Francisco: City Lights Books, 1984.

Vornberger, William, ed. *Fire from the Sky: A Collection of Salvadoran Children's Drawings.* New York: Writer's and Readers Publishing Cooperative, 1986.

INDEX

ABOUT THE AUTHOR

Karen Schwabach currently lives with her dog, Chester, in Chefornak, Alaska. Her home has electricity but no running water. Chefornak has no roads or cars and can only be reached by plane. Ms. Schwabach teaches English as a Second Language to Yup'ik Eskimo children in the village school. She is also the author of *Thailand: Land of Smiles*.